THE CANCER WHISPERER'S

RECOVERY GUIDE

THE CANCER WHISPERER'S RECOVERY GUIDE

CURE IS WITHIN

DR. MELANIE ERCEG

ISBN 13: 978-1-941768-01-3

Dedicated to
Margaret Rankin
1933 - 2000

Do not unwrap until the 22nd century when ready to feel responsible.

Data
What We Already Know:

- Stress is a main precursor in autoimmune disorders such as cancer.

- The way we care for ourselves, our bodies, and manage our lives creates either stressful or relaxing physiological responses.

- Human beings can control the stress response and the relaxation response.

- You are human.

- As a human you have the power to create changes in your body, negative and positive, which result in death or life.

Since we already know the body is the result of consciousness, this puts us in an optimal position. The old days of victimization wherein we mistook the body for an enemy over which we had no control or influence, are over. We have been living in a society that has mostly forgotten love, except in romance. We have forgotten love having to do with time and nurture, and even pace with the rhythm of life, which shows up as disease in a number of people.

Since disease of mind or body means disease in consciousness (thoughts, beliefs, and treatment from the self toward the self) manifesting as a block in chi/ki/energy, the solution involves changing the patterns that led to the result. Oftentimes this includes a healthy, active parenting style within.

Life is relationships. The relationship we have with ourselves, our relationships with our family, friends, and colleagues all mirror our inner relationship, such as how we structure our time, give and receive, form boundaries, and commit to agreements.

A key component in many aspects of life is responsibility: choosing how we contribute to society, our role in a family, and of course, taking care of our bodies.

Reading these pages, as anything we read in life, the final hour depends on whether we apply it. This often relates to worth, choosing to make decisions for the highest benefit. Life: action required.

Keyword is responsibility, which relates to empowerment.

Hashtag isn't judgment.
It is responsibility.

Being responsible places us in the position of power.

We had the power to adversely affect our health, just as we have the power to heal it through an overall far-reaching change of the way we have run our lives.

It is cause and effect.
Give and receive.
Action and reaction.
Even gene potentiality, as we'll learn, is malleable. The brain is capable of functional reorganization throughout the course of our lives.

Doctors who have graduated to the level of inspecting the mind's role in health examine genes to reach the same conclusion: biologically, we are not genetically predetermined to suffer the way other people's cells in our family might have. It depends on the mind in the body.

The caveat in science is that generally we have to wait about a hundred years for old ideas to be released from the knuckles of scientists who became attached to them.

Regardless, we can heal intelligently in our lives. People in the modern day use well-known holistic techniques to heal.

Changing Times

Increasingly more people are healing illness using the holistic approach. In modern times, many of us are choosing the empowered route in health, albeit through ancient practices. Many books detail recoveries occurring without using old methods, which may have been tied up in business arrangements with the hospital.

It is understandable that in the past we used liquid toxins or machines to try to fix the illness. When we didn't understand cancer, we made corresponding choices. Through this guidebook, by understanding what it is, the ability to heal comes within your reach.

We honor former generations doing the best they could with what they knew at that time. Perhaps our grandparents ate a lot of bird mucous, such as eggs or cow byproducts, thus creating an acidic cellular environment. Although cancer is found in such environments, it has more to do with mental and emotional patterns.

Perhaps prior generations led sedentary lifestyles, or felt powerless to change. We love and embrace people unconditionally while healing gracefully in our lives.

Cancer

As identified, the cure is within. Curing cancer involves a multidisciplinary approach of actively loving and parenting the self. You must.

The degree to which this affects the body is that amidst neglect, the body begins to foreclose and cancer happens. It is a completely new way of thinking. Before, we thought cancer happened to us. We were stricken or victimized.

Learning to take care of yourself is a process. Earth is a school wherein we learn. Through these weeks, you will learn how to direct the course of your health and take care of yourself.

The body is the expression and result of how it is being treated by the self. If the body is starting to die, it evidently isn't pleased by how it is being treated by the self. When neglect and being out of rhythm with ourselves became common, cancer became common.

Since cancer is the unnurtured child/body/receiver of treatment from the self toward the self, healing entails doing the opposite.

Each ailment in itself is the gift showing what you've been up to, and is rooted in a specific, ongoing pattern. We already know cancer is long-standing resentment within the self from how it is being treated by the self.

Since people with cancer are among the nicest people we know, resentment is usually from an unnourished inner self, nourishing everyone in the world except oneself.

Largely these ways that we treat ourselves are under the radar of our conscious awareness: unconscious.

We may not mean to hurt ourselves, therefore the body is there to show us. If we wash rayon or cashmere in water, it shrinks. We didn't mean to hurt the top. It was a learning experience. We find a better way.

When a pet is not fed and shrivels, and it was ours to care of, we meet the result. When our unnurtured self has had enough and expresses itself in the form of cancer, we definitely wake up and reevaluate our priorities.

Though the information here seems plainly evident, it wouldn't be to a society out of rhythm with itself.

"Huh?" might be the response. Exactly. Providing love, care, and nourishment within is absolutely at the heart of health.

During your stay on Earth, you have been given a body to take care of. You are the parent of the body, the child.

Regardless of whether you have separate children, the parent-child relationship within reigns supreme. It is the template through which you form all your relationships, mirroring how you treat yourself.

Respecting yourself, appreciating the body as sacred, and creating fun and joy in your world is a choice benefitting health. Another choice is its opposite, resulting in opposite health. It's really your call. Each attitude creates corresponding results.

Was the search for a cure just a road leading outside of us? Was the remedy to abdicate power, to run? Or was it to acknowledge our power as cause creating effect?

As it turned out, the cure wasn't to run away. Our body is the result showing us our treatment. The search has ended. You are found, with the power to treat yourself kindly and respectfully, with dignity.

Yes, tomatoes, Chernobyl or other environmental factors can be labeled as culprits, yet not everyone smoking gets lung cancer, for example. Other factors are at play.

Pollution on Earth reflects our consciousness on a global scale. Our mental and emotional patterns cause results in the body. How we handle emotion-generating circumstances directly affects the immune system.

When an abundance of stress is recorded by the limbic system, the hypothalamus causes the pituitary gland to throw off the endocrine system, which is in charge of hormonal balance. During this imbalance, an increase in abnormal cells can easily occur.

The hypothalamus also controls the immune system so that the immune system is suppressed at precisely the time abnormal cell reproduction is at its highest. This we call cancer, and we can reverse what we created and return to health.

Forms of stress vary from running around, too busy for the self, ongoing lack of self- care, emotional feelings left unprocessed, the list goes on. We already know stress is a main cause in autoimmune disorders like cancer. The body is the story of your life.

In the weeks to come, you will be writing a new story, aligned with your desire for health. You will be enjoying your vegetable smoothies, avoiding meat and sugar to maintain an alkaline system, feeling and clearing, bringing laughter into your world, and caring for yourself. We are starting at the most fundamental level because it is the root. Well done on making the first step on your path to health. Your courage is commendable.

The receiving (body) part of you is experiencing a result.
Balancing the inner parent-child relationship sustains health.
The parent is the giver of treatment: Give that which you want to receive.

45 Day Program

WEEK 1

Day 1

Consciousness is a set of beliefs and perceptions about ourselves and the world. You choose your consciousness through free will.

Understanding you are causal in your life is a relief endowing you with the ability to manage your life. Begin by spending 15 minutes contemplating the following statement, once in the morning and again at night:

Consciousness will, in fact, change the desired outcome.

Day 2

Feel and say the following during waking hours:

I can. I believe I can. I can change. I am willing to change.

Day 3

What is it you most want to see happen in the world? For example, do you want all starving children to be fed?

_____

_____

_____

_____

_____

_____

_____

_____

_____

_____

_____

_____

_____

_____

What do you wish more people were like?

_____

_____

_____

_____

_____

_____

_____

_____

_____

_____

_____

_____

_____

_____

Day 4

See yourself giving that change to yourself and to whomever else.

Day 5

Today, be the change you want to see in the world.

Well done!

Day 6

Observe your inner dialogue. Observe you are creating it.

In the afternoon, consider you are the parent to your own child, the body. Write down the attributes you want your child to learn. Do you want your child to succeed in health? Feel loved? Be confident and capable?

_____

_____

_____

_____

_____

_____

_____

_____

_____

_____

_____

_____

_____

_____

Shift your inner dialogue. Be the parent. Instill these values. Give praise within to your own daughter/son self. This is the inner cycle, the healthy parent-child/ give-receive cycle within.

Day 7

A natural sense of gratitude and fortitude is developing within you. While feeling grateful, see, know, and feel the wonderful changes that are happening within you.

Find all the funny material you can, since laughter is the best medicine. It moves energy. Through these weeks, when you are finished with the day's lesson, engage in laughter.

WEEK 2

Day 8

Praise and Strengthening Self Worth

What kind of dialogue are you aware of?

_____

_____

_____

_____

_____

_____

_____

_____

_____

Do you feel strong enough to reteach yourself? Why or why not?

_____

_____

_____

_____

_____

_____

_____

_____

_____

Are you committed to parenting yourself to health?

_____

_____

_____

_____

_____

_____

Strengthening the Belief that You Can
Practice vocalizing:

I am worthy, able to effect lasting change.
I am a powerful person.
It is appropriate for me to use my power to positively affect my health.

Regardless of excuses that may surface, it is your task to understand that they were based in an old mentality. You are creating a new, healthy dialogue within.

Great job on the implementation of new healthy patterns!

Day 9

Opening to the New
Can you open up, raise your arms high in the air and let love in? Why or why not?

_____

_____

_____

_____

_____

_____

_____

_____

_____

_____

_____

If good news walked up to you, would you be able to hear it?

_____

_____

_____

_____

_____

_____

_____

_____

_____

_____

Everyone has reasons to be happy or not. It is a choice, based on self worth. What do you want? It is a free will decision.

_____

_____

_____

_____

_____

_____

_____

_____

_____

_____

Being a Giver and Receiver Within Cycles of Love
High evolution is love. Free up to let creative expression flow through.

Life is here in all its majestic beauty, refinement, and raw power.

It is here, where are you?

_____

_____

_____

_____

_____

_____

_____

_____

_____

Abundance is from a large awareness. It is natural. If sensing abundance is not the natural picture of your awareness, then visualize it.

Visualization is from consciousness, which stems from worth. Worth is based on how you treat yourself.

Making time for real enjoyment is part of parenting yourself. Parenting/giving can be as subtle as bringing a loving gaze into your heart, taking a deep breath, or centering. In what ways do you parent/give to the receiving part of yourself?

_____

_____

_____

_____

_____

_____

_____

_____

_____

_____

As follows, how do you share and give to others?

_____

_____

_____

_____

_____

_____

_____

_____

_____

Humans are on a journey to remember their God-ness, true energy, real self.

Day 10

The vernacular for cancer in the past revolved around tissues and genes. It examined external and internal risk factors, how to control them and how to fight against them.

The new reality is to lift our heads from the microscope and understand how we shape our health. When we study the Laws of the Universe, have we come across the Law of Victimization? Or do we more frequently hear of the Law of Free Will?

Studying the dynamics of what we once thought cancer was, contained victimization in the loop of: deflection (other people's genes), the Earth's atmosphere (environmental), and food.

These all play a role. Yet, the stronger impact comes from within. What we choose to ingest stems from our consciousness. The field of psychoneuroimmunology (meaning the mind and body are linked) provides evidentiary support as to how we create both debilitating and invigorating results in the body.

What about Genetics?
We used to think that we were victims of our genes and had no free will. We would research from an angle that found our organs out of control, doing things to us, the victims.
Because the medical industry makes billions each year, self-healing has not been widely publicized.

It may seem true that we are genetically predetermined to suffer the same health problems as our mother, because she got cancer and then we got cancer, too. However, this is only a potential.

It increases in likelihood if we unconsciously run the same energy that we learned from her, such as the trait of holding in feelings, thereby creating energetic blocks.

It is true that we are predisposed to experience the same types of manifestations as those around us, if we copy their behavior. Sometimes, we continue the same patterns and suffer the same consequences, such as the same illnesses.

The body is the effect of consciousness. Consciousness is first, creating physical results. Remember the key word, responsibility. Just because one person is holding onto resentment, or not taking care of the self, does not mean we need to. Could accusing genetics be a polite way of saying, "My health is somebody else's fault?"

Studies About Genetics: Neural Plasticity

In the past few decades, discoveries in neurobiology reveal that our experiences not only affect our moods, but also physically change our brain structure and functions through the course of our lives. This is referred to as neural plasticity.

It was originally studied by Nobel Prize winners in Medicine, David Hubel and Torsten Wiesel in 1981.

As we experience life with its emotion-producing events, our reactions, such as our feelings and the way we process events, act upon our brain and transform its structure.

While we may theoretically say that we are genetically predisposed to certain possibilities, the brain is capable of elaborate, functional reorganization throughout our entire lives.

Our feelings affect our bodies, including our brains. We have now found this to be biochemically true. Experience changes us. The way it changes us is that our reactions alter the synaptic connections and neuronal density of our brains. The brain is continuing to modify itself according to incoming stimuli.*

It is not a sentimental notion that our feelings affect our brain chemistry. It is true. We are not the victims of our bodies.

*Documented in: *Welcome to Earth, Answers to Life Questions*

Compassionate Responsibility: Releasing the Old Illusion of Victimization

Compassionately ask yourself the following:

Can I make a clear distinction between blame and responsibility?

_____

_____

_____

_____

_____

_____

_____

_____

_____

_____

_____

Can I release blame? Can I transform blame into capability?

_____

_____

_____

_____

_____

_____

_____

_____

_____

_____

_____

_____

Can I feel responsible without judgment?

_____
_____
_____
_____
_____
_____
_____
_____
_____
_____
_____
_____
_____
_____

Can I observe with compassion?

_____
_____
_____
_____
_____
_____
_____
_____
_____
_____
_____
_____
_____
_____

Can I feel good, knowing that the power is in my hands? Can I feel happy, learning of this power I have, and learning how to use it to create what I want?

_____
_____
_____
_____
_____
_____
_____
_____
_____
_____

In what ways did I think I was a victim?

_____
_____
_____
_____
_____
_____
_____
_____
_____
_____

In what ways do I feel powerful?

_____
_____
_____
_____
_____

_____
_____
_____
_____
_____

How can these two ideas find balance?

_____
_____
_____
_____
_____
_____
_____
_____
_____
_____

The Rescuer-Victim Cycle
Rescuers seek victims to try to heal their own inner victim. As they heal, they define the boundary. They make the distinction that they are responsible for everything in their lives, and other people are responsible for their own lives.

Exploration
In what ways do I abdicate responsibility?

_____
_____
_____
_____
_____

_____
_____
_____
_____
_____

In what ways do I feel responsibility?

_____
_____
_____
_____
_____
_____
_____
_____
_____
_____

Bridging the Divide
Without a doubt, the universe is constantly showing us the way it works.

Since we are always creating our lives and reactions from free will, we can learn to become aware of the subtle layers in our consciousness. The body is here to point out our consciousness.

Exploratory Questions
Can I let go of the judgment that I may have been unaware of until now?

_____
_____
_____

_____

_____

_____

_____

_____

_____

_____

Am I willing to consider changing the patterns for the benefit of my health?

_____

_____

_____

_____

_____

_____

_____

_____

_____

For the benefit of my health and those around me, am I willing to change beliefs of disempowerment into true empowerment?

_____

_____

_____

_____

_____

_____

_____

_____

_____

Which new beliefs sustain my health?

_____

_____

_____

_____

_____

_____

_____

_____

_____

_____

Fill your mind with this new data upon rising and going to sleep.

Day 11

Power

In the past, we may have interpreted power as force. Yet, consider the nature of a martial art such as Aikido, where we use the strength of the opponent to our advantage. Can we use the same ideology on our road back to health?

Am I willing to use my power?

_____

_____

_____

_____

_____

_____

_____

_____

_____

_____

_____

If no, what do I think may happen if I use my power to its full capability?

_____

_____

_____

_____

_____

_____

_____

_____

_____

_____

Is this true?

_____

_____

_____

_____

_____

_____

_____

_____

_____

_____

If I am not sure why I have not been using power to recognize my role in health and healing, can I forgive myself?

_____

_____

_____

_____

_____

_____

_____

_____

_____

Forgive the past. Today is new. Allow deep waves of understanding to move through your being and out of it, feeling refreshed, and lightened.

Days 12 and 13

Vocalize the Affirmations:

I am using my power to affect my health beneficially.

I am comfortable directing my power into matters that improve health.

Your subconscious is there to receive and implement the data.

Well done!

Day 14

Cross Reference

As we steer ourselves back on the road of health, let us specifically examine where the block developed.

Each organ in the body pertains to specific energy or personality patterns. The throat relates to expression. The liver stores anger. The lungs relates to worth, and our ability to open and receive life.

Cancer represents long term resentment from the self to the self for not being taken care of. If it manifests in the breast, which represents nourishment, the equation would read: resentment at being denied nourishment. Its solution is to provide it.

These patterns have been unconscious, and therefore manifest physically as a sign to heal the manifestation's corresponding causative pattern. This is discussed in the Medicine Chapter of *Welcome to Earth, Answers to Life Questions.*

A complete list of common personality patterns and their solution affirmations to transform is found in Louise Hay's, *Heal Your Body A-Z.* You can also google Louise Hay and the organ, and will likely find the new thought-pattern to heal it.

Say the new pattern. The subconscious easily accepts the new data upon consistency and sincerity.

Where is your disease manifesting? In which organ or area?

_____

_____

_____

_____

_____

_____

_____

_____

_____

_____

_____

_____

_____

_____

_____

Acknowledge the mental pattern that created it:

_____

_____

_____

_____

_____

_____

_____

_____

_____

_____

Continue giving your subconscious the data of the new healthy pattern found in the list of the latter book.

Week 3

Day 15

As Above, So Below

Consider how we bless a meal, thanking the sun, rain, earth, and air for playing their roles. Our food is literally created by each element.

The plant thrives from each of these elements causing it to grow, flourish, and sustain its health. Would the plant thrive without any sun? How about without any rain? No air? No roots?

Let us explore how each of these components are representations within ourselves and the foundation of health.

The sun's gaze of warmth represents our loving gaze within. It is the heart. Our bodies respond, as we provide time to realign into a state of calm, and shine this loving gaze within.

Air represents our ability to take in breath, and to receive life through breath. As this becomes automatic, we sustain health by remaining open, giving and receiving life.

The rain is the water we need to live. It also represents the cleansing of our emotions. As we let go of old emotions, we are cleansed and renewed.

The earth represents grounding in the physical body. By leaving the mind's chatter, we are deeply grounded in the calm center of ourselves.

Make an agreement with yourself to provide these components that are necessary for health. As you practice each element within, your body respond gratefully with vibrant health.

Day 16

Months prior to the onset of the disease, what happened in your life, if anything?

_____

_____

_____

_____

_____

_____

_____

_____

_____

_____

How do you manage stress?

_____

_____

_____

_____

_____

_____

_____

_____

_____
_____
_____

What steps do you currently take to foster relaxation so that your body is releasing positive hormones that benefit your health?

_____
_____
_____
_____
_____
_____
_____
_____
_____
_____
_____
_____

Is your life set up in a way that nurtures all aspects of you?

_____
_____
_____
_____
_____
_____
_____
_____
_____
_____
_____
_____

Day 17

Let's Set It Up

Draw a five point star. This is your relationship with self and others. Each point represents a different aspect of your relationships:

- Relationship with self, including meditating, spiritual practices, feeling and clearing emotions, and nurturing time.

- Relationship with others, including family and community.

- Creativity.

- Career.

- Add your own unique point.

Trace the star and label each point:

Day 18

Application

Include all the aspects you require for fulfillment and organize a schedule in your life to fulfill. Remember, we are the parents of our lives. The body is the receiver of the treatment.

Do you believe you have the right to be happy? Why or why not?

_____

_____

_____

_____

_____

_____

_____

_____

_____

_____

_____

Write your old conceptions about the way you thought life had to be:

_____

_____

_____

_____

_____

_____

_____

_____

_____

_____

_____

We are all deserving. We have all played roles of light and dark. Do you believe you deserve to be happy, nurtured, and fulfilled?

_____

_____

_____

_____

_____

_____

_____

_____

_____

_____

_____

_____

Transform any illusions that life had to be un-nurturing to survive. Let go of and release all prior illusions.

Form new healthy commitments to yourself to inspire your being, restoring your health. Write your commitments to yourself:

_____

_____

_____

_____

_____

_____

_____

_____

_____

_____

_____

_____

_____

_____

Practice at least two nourishing practices from your relationship with the self. Write your experience and response to the last exercise.

_____

_____

_____

_____

_____

_____

_____

_____

_____

_____

_____

If the feelings do not have words, let these feelings surround you, and infiltrate your being.

Day 19

Forgiveness of Past: Forgiving People and Ways of Treating the Self

Consider that people who upset you played roles of darkness to help you see, by reflecting unseen parts of the self. As we know, the universe (us) sends pictures in the form of people and circumstances, to show us our own consciousness, which makes for easier forgiveness. It is merely an acknowledgment and recognition of self.

Forgiveness means appreciating the role someone played to get us to see our consciousness. Which people could you not forgive? What were their traits?

_____

_____

_____
_____
_____
_____
_____
_____
_____
_____
_____
_____
_____

Without judgment, realize those who trigger us most reflect unseen, unconscious parts within,. Take a moment to transform these traits into their opposites and treat yourself this way:

_____
_____
_____
_____
_____
_____
_____
_____
_____
_____
_____
_____
_____
_____

Facing the Body
This step involves thanking the body for showing us what we were doing before it was too late. Thank it for communicating to you so that you may open your eyes to see. Forgive the body.

Forgiving the Self

How was your treatment of the self today? Did you structure to make time for your favorite things that create happiness for you?

_____

_____

_____

_____

_____

_____

_____

_____

_____

_____

_____

_____

_____

_____

_____

_____

Renew with strength and dedication the resolve to treat the self right.

Practice two or more actions pertaining to your new life from the star, as part of your nurturing system within you.

Prayerful Thanksgiving

It doesn't matter if you are spiritual, or religious, or not. All your thoughts are a prayer. Out into the universe they travel and reflect back to you.

Energy runs a cycle, as life is cyclical. Seasons continue returning, year after year. Your feelings and attitudes come back to you in kind.

Day 20

Self Care Organization Schedule
All elements are in place. Are you practicing nourishing all aspects of your self in your life? Share your experience:

_____
_____
_____
_____
_____
_____
_____
_____
_____
_____
_____
_____
_____

Positiveness vs. Realness
Statistics import that a surprising number of people had cancer in Marin, a region of very positive folk, and of course the environment reflects consciousness.

Being positive is splendid. Leaving unprocessed feelings inside isn't. It monumentally affects health.

On TV, when we see visitors in the cancer ward, they are definitely having a great experience because everyone is so positive.

It is nice to spread love. In addition, we make our own private time to process feelings so they flow through us and out. It is equally healthy to feel the love through us as it envelops the world.

Is it okay to feel what I'm feeling, or do I want to show only a positive face?

_____

_____

_____

_____

_____

_____

_____

_____

_____

_____

_____

_____

Do I take time to myself to acknowledge the feeling and heal it?

_____

_____

_____

_____

_____

_____

_____

_____

_____

_____

_____

Here is the challenge: release fear or blame, turn inward and face ourselves with understanding and compassion. We'll elaborate on this next week.

WEEK 4

Day 22

Positive Protons and Negative Electrons Are Both Found in a Healthy Cell

Cancer thrives in an acidic environment. It is better to have mainly alkaline chemistry.

Blood has a good pH at 7.35 - 7.45 in humans. The GI system secretes acids to digest food, returning to a neutral pH afterwards.

Homeostasis optimizes the body. If too acidic you take yourself out of that balance. (Breathing) oxygen is another way to maintain your equilibrium.

A chemically positive substance is missing electrons. So too, the dark must be felt for balance.

Examples include feeling sadness or any feeling by acknowledging and transforming. Running from them just leaves them inside your body, blocking chi flow and creating cancer.

Feelings must be felt in order to be transcended. More impacting than being positive, is being yourself.

Experience your feeling, observing them in the body. Let them come up. Feel them. Allow them to be felt fully and compassionately. Let them transmute, and they exit. Repeat throughout life.

Acknowledging the feelings by meditating on parts of your body where the energy has accumulated allows the energy to dissipate. It is a matter of gently bringing the focus within.

See meditation found in appendix, next to the spleen, or in the back of book.

Day 23

Nutrition

Ingesting vegetables, which are alkaline, rather than meat and sugar, which are acidic, is part of a whole-spectrum health plan. Processing emotions is another part of the spectrum. Consulting an Ayurvedic practitioner (resource at end of book) is also useful in determining relevant herbs. For example, milk thistle is healing for the liver. Choosing plant-based proteins is appropriate. Hemp powder is a well balanced omega source.

Return to the star. Take care of yourself. Caring for the self and being loving by acknowledging feelings comes first. Everything else will fall into place after that. You'll see.

⚜ ⚜ ⚜

Remember a time the body showed you what you were doing. Watch and know your cancer is dissolving as you acknowledge and shift into healthy patterns.

See your organ filling with light. This light is coming from you, in your awareness. Appreciate the organ. Tell it thank you.

Use creative visualization. Appreciate your body and all the joy it brings.

Day 24

The Relaxation Response
The amygdala in your brain triggers the fight or flight response by releasing cortisol. Alternately, if you are generating calmness, your brain produces endorphins from feeling relaxed. This happens when we breathe deeply or repeat a mantra.

It's a great example of how you have the power to influence your body. We do it all the time. It is about becoming conscious, so that instead of being passive or helpless, you use techniques to produce the results you want in health.

Smiling Meditation to Organs
Begin with a deep breath. In the darkness of the universe, imagine a sun glowing. It is beaming at your heart. See it, feel it. Spend as much time as needed feeling it. It fills you with love and healing.

Now that your heart is lit up, it is ready to light up all the other organs in your body through its loving, beaming power. Move through your body, paying special attention to the organs that need it the most. This can be done while sitting or taking a walk.

Day 25

Check over your organization structure. See if you want to add anything.

Are any revisions necessary? Have you thought of new ways to nourish your being? Include and apply:

_____

_____

_____

_____
_____
_____
_____
_____
_____
_____

Express gratitude for the wonderful changes taking place in your body. These come from you. You are dong it. You are making change happen in your body.

Excellent work!

Day 26

Community Support
The benefit of community cannot be underestimated. Find people who support you on your path. Meet with a doctor or healer who believes in you, and the power to heal.

Loneliness can be stressful. The good news is that you can do something about it. There are always people who like what you like. Google a group of likeminded people and join them. Having people to talk to is healing.

Day 27

Your Life is a Prayer.
Love is the natural essence. Remembering has been part of our journey. From a mass consciousness point of view, it is time to release suffering. Causing love is proactive. There is so much joy around us if we tune into it, forgive, and let go.

Practice letting go of material from your awareness each day. Let new revitalizing energy infiltrate your being in its place, lightening you.

I let go of that which no longer serves. I let go of:

_____
_____
_____
_____
_____
_____
_____
_____
_____
_____
_____
_____
_____
_____
_____
_____
_____
_____
_____

Day 28

Joyful Thanksgiving
Express gratitude for everything you can think of, even the things that bother you, because it all has a silver lining:

_____
_____
_____

_____

_____

_____

_____

_____

_____

_____

_____

_____

_____

_____

_____

_____

_____

_____

Meditation: I am a unique individual with the power to shape my life. I am making decisions that match my right to live in happiness. I am happier to help any other family members or friends by taking care of myself, so that I am filled up first and able. Everyday I feel better. I am comfortable using my power to change my health. I am thankful.

WEEK 5

Caregiver Patient
Parent Child
Teacher Student

These inherent models all begin within. As our own parent-child cycle, we take care of ourselves, giving time and nourishment within.

Only we can create a life appropriate to fulfill our needs. Our choices depend on how we feel about ourselves.

Worth
You are worthy!
The world has been peppered with a plethora of people who have forgotten their basic self-worth. As you recall your worth, you take care of yourself appropriately.
You are worth the love.

This week, take time to parent your worth.
You are raising your own body child.
As a good parent you teach self worth.

Return to the star. Is your life taking on the form of fulfillment by your fulfilling it?

Check your schedule. Are you making time for your needs to be met?

Shift the structure as to allow implementation of the star points. You are organizing your week to meet your needs. If you meet any resistance, listen and feel it. Parent it through compassionately hearing, and directing the flow to your highest vision of health, including reminding yourself of your inherent worth:

_____

_____

_____

_____

_____

_____

_____

_____

_____

_____

_____

_____

_____

_____

_____

_____

_____

_____

_____

_____

_____

WEEK 6

Treatment
Each day incorporate healthy, supportive treatment of yourself.

Directing Energy
This life is your directorial debut. As a soul infusing a body, you have the power and free will create your life, affect your health, and provide care.

Treatment of Self
Consider that you are in this world, on earth in this life, in charge of taking care of a child – you. You're only a relatively few feet tall so it's perfect that you acknowledge this body is yours to take care of, nourish, and support: mentally, physically, emotionally, and if you're open to it, spiritually.

Support yourself as you would a friend. You're the one to take a friend's side. If you want to lose a friend you, criticize or chastise that friend.

Yet you probably don't do that to your friends, so why would you to that yourself, your friend?

_____
_____
_____
_____

_____

_____

_____

_____

_____

_____

Common Subtle Mistreatment
- At end of task instead of praise and boundaries, doing more than agreed upon.
- No deep breathing.
- Lungs relate to worth - our ability to take in life
- No thought discipline
- No grounding procedures

With compassion, begin to apologize for the past ways of treating self: i.e. the rushing, not giving time, etc., even if you didn't realize it.

Next step: forgiveness. You were doing best you could.

_____

_____

_____

_____

_____

_____

_____

_____

_____

_____

_____

_____

New Healthy, Supportive Treatment of Self
Meditation can be done for a few minutes upon awakening. It is a multifaceted, rich experience. Purporting time restraints is a construct or idea, made by us. We form the rhythm of our society collectively. The rich among us have lots of time, dividing it appropriately.

Grounding procedures
From the dan tien, just below the navel, create your grounding cord to the center of the earth. This will help you stay grounded and focused.

Clearing and Protection of Your Energetic Field
We are all energy. Just as we shower, we also clear the energy field through a process best suited for the individual. I.e. running light through the 7 auric layers, providing a protective shield around yourself energetically.

Chakras can be cleared through your own procedure or by rotating, moving, vacuuming and filling with light. More information on energetic layers is described in NASA physicist, Barbara Brennan's, books.

Inner Approval, "I approve of you exactly as you are right now."
Praise.
Rather than shutting out the self when working, invite yourself to be there, aware of what you are doing.

Doing something incredibly boring that you think inner self wouldn't be interested in? Why are you doing it? There are many avenues through which your real self can express.

Treating the self at the caliber at which you resonate, i.e. a weekly schedule accounting for your needs, love, types of food you register with. It is a process. Moving to healthy, water-filled foods is a result and cause of health.

Time for Your Own World
Music, natural springs, prayer, whatever it is, carve a section in the day to fulfill it.
Breathe. Give time for full breathing. Open, and let it in.

Look in the mirror into your own eyes.
This is the showdown.

Facing the self,
Look into your eyes,
Let go.

Perceive that you are the parent, looking into the eyes of the receiver part of you, the way you've been treating yourself. Make contact. See your own eyes. Repeat through life. Engage. You're having a relationship.

Let tears flow as it will probably come to this.
It is the beginning, the meeting. Everything is uphill from here.

The receiving part of you speaks through the body.

Be Able to See Ghosts
No, but try to be aware of the responses of your real self through intuition.

In time you'll perceive your "self" through honoring your feelings that are palpably flowing through you. By acknowledging, you're making better decisions, staying healthy, honoring boundaries, and being there for those you love.

Make sure life is funny. If not, make it so, through shifting your lens.

Try bringing your eyes down to heart level. It will relax you.

Incorporate these elements into your daily life. You can do it. You are healthy.

Giving in the world begins with giving inside oneself. You become the walking example. World healing has to do with one person, the self.

Each of us can do it. This is the parent-child cycle operational within. A healthy relationship within staves off illness, fills you with love, makes you feel good, and creates a positive impact on those around you.

Free Will
We are not defined by a steadfast non-change.
We are ever-changing, adapting to situations, and using our free will.

Using your will releases you from victimization, knowing that everything you need is inside of you, as part of the universe.

Who Are We?
If we already know the universe is holographic; the whole is contained within each part, as each part contains the whole, and are aware that there is fundamentally one energy and we are it, whether we call this God, energy, spirit, or matter, it is clear that we are all of the same source/energy. God is having an experience as (insert name).

Love
Through all the years of research and searching, beyond the seeking, behind the test tubes, was love. This ingredient, so essential and normal, is the substance holding the universe together and your body. The body speaks to be taken care of. We know what's

real, and no amount of denying love's power will heal us fully in the long term.

Is it possible that the remedy to victimization is opening up and providing?

As we open, accessing the vast God-ness/energy that is everywhere, feeling filled with love within, it is then easy to give/parent. One of the ways to access is through meditation.

Appendix

Meditative Practice

Data Usage: Too many thoughts is costly to your health. Meditation provides a calm space to produce your relaxation response, thereby encouraging positive brain and immune responses.

If love is all around us, where are you?
Let's GPS and find you.

Wherever you went, let's now bring you back into alignment. Through breath or shifting your awareness, begin the meditation.

We can do many things in meditation, connect with /as source, let thoughts go, or guide the experience intentionally.

For this practice, let's bring the focus inside. Eyes drop down within self.
Make a connection again with yourself by feeling the essence of your body.

Any areas of discomfort are there to gain your focus through the discomfort, so simply bring your loving focus to these places, and the discomfort eventually dissolves. Take all the time you need.

Resources

Technology and Apps
In Europe, a breathalyzer app is being developed for early detection. Digital breast screening detects breast cancer without the radiation of a mammogram. The point though, is to take care of yourself.

Dietary/ Herbal Support
During this time, an Ayurvedic practitioner is useful. Consider practicalayurveda.com. Familiar with the quality of this person, he can work with anyone worldwide with various complex issues.

Healing Support
The healing process can run deep. It is helpful to work with a counselor to help you navigate and heal. To schedule a counseling session or find the right healer for you, contact Dr. Melanie. *beingwellwithmel.com*
Parenting info is found in the Parenting chapter of *Welcome to Earth, Answers to Life Questions.*

To rid cancer would be to rid the result of how we (unconsciously) treated ourselves.

Parenting, loving self, creates solid worth. Go to > Louise Hay's chart in *Heal Your Body A-Z* to integrate corresponding organ data.

It is that simple when we release victimization and align with empowerment.

Parenting means giving that which we want to receive, within and in the world.

Ridding cancer = getting people to love themselves. Living our lives is learning how to love. Evolution seldom rushes.

In the end, one lets go to realize, this is the Earth planet, with a civilization journeying through a forgotten true essence of god-ness. On the journey, forgetting is part of it all. Every level is fine. It is the path to remembrance.

We can show up on Earth, write books, remind of our inherent alignment with/as source.

Ultimately we each remember for ourselves, perhaps time down the line.

Only when we feel it, will it ring true.

People come and go, on and off the planet, speak truth, share experiences. We touch each other's lives for sure, and when we are ready we wake up.

It has been such a blessing having been here, to feel, to interact with our fellow souls. We are all so similar, so much more the same than different. Our uniqueness was so lovely to see.

May we find peace in remembrance, back into the whole of all that is.

Namaste

Printed in Great Britain
by Amazon

75643635R00040